WINTER GARDEN

Jardín de Invierno

PABLO NERUDA

Winter Garden

TRANSLATED BY WILLIAM O'DALY

COPPER CANYON PRESS : PORT TOWNSEND

Poems from *Winter Garden* have appeared
in *American Poetry Review* and *Another Chicago Magazine*.

Publication of this book was made possible by a grant
from the National Endowment for the Arts.

Copper Canyon Press is in residence with Centrum
at Fort Worden State Park.

Special thanks to Stephanie Lutgring.

ISBN 0-914742-99-X (cloth)
ISBN 0-914742-93-0
Library of Congress Catalog Card Number 86-71837

Cover: Galen Garwood, monotype (*Centrum Press*).

COPPER CANYON PRESS
Post Office Box 271
Port Townsend
Washington 98368

CONTENTS

INTRODUCTION

Winter Garden, the third book in Copper Canyon's Neruda Series, was among the eight unpublished manuscripts which lay on the poet's desk on the day of his death in September, 1973. Neruda wrote no book more direct and passionate in its language, and yet as rich in subtlety, in the modulation of music and image, in the fine warp and woof of his vision of the planet's life. No book of his contains more genuine love for what nourished him, and in no other book does he more clearly define his commitment to himself and to others. His responsibilities to his people (sometimes Chileans and sometimes all people) were the challenge that made him a poet. They were also the burden that he carried in his solitude. But in solitude, his ability to restore himself and to clarify his loves strengthened over the years, as his aloneness was transformed from being the enemy in *Residencias I & II* (1925-1935) to being a faithful companion in *Winter Garden*. The poet enjoyed nothing more than the abundant wildflowers and the birds of Isla Negra's winter coastline, where with his wife, Matilde Urrutia, he made the home closest to his heart.

In 1971 he left his beloved Chile to be her ambassador to France. Dying of cancer, he undertook the mission as he had most of his other political and diplomatic ventures: with a sense of fulfilling his duty and his destiny. He shared with one of his literary grandfathers, Francisco de Quevedo, an attraction for life in motion, with all of its changes and contradictions and contrasts. Like the Baroque poet, he rarely could deny his political commitments or his social conscience. Still, the journey must have been in part a journey away from himself, away from what made him happiest. And, as always during his absences, Chile became more lovely to him wherever he went. He was a poet who grew outward to meet the challenge of his people, to embrace and distance himself from their great love and their indifference, to accept the gifts of his life and his death with the dignity of a man who little by little built for himself a home on earth. Of his last days, which fell in the two weeks after the military coup that the poet himself had foreseen, Fernando Alegría writes: "...Neruda, wide-eyed, bearded now, wants to see all this death, and pulling himself halfway up, suddenly knows that at last he is 'face to face with the truth.' "

In this book, he greets us with a mixture of affection and candor, and keeps his privacy. He invites us into his home and allows us to make it our own, while he retires to his study or goes for a walk beside the winter sea.

WILLIAM O'DALY
July 1986

ACKNOWLEDGMENTS

I would like to thank my colleague Dr. Sergio Bocaz-Moraga, Professor of Modern Languages at Eastern Washington University, for once again giving me the generous gift of his energy and time. I am also indebted to Cecilia Vicuña, Chilean poet and editor, whose careful clarifications and suggestions benefited the translation. I recommend Manuel Duran's and Margery Safir's *Earth Tones* as a solid primer for anyone interested in learning more about Pablo Neruda and his poetry. In a couple of instances, I could find no better way of translating passages of *Winter Garden* than they already had. And I want to thank their book for steering me to Fernando Alegría's *Neruda: Reminiscences and Critical Reflections*, from which I borrowed the quotation that appears in the introduction. Any lapses in the translation of *Winter Garden* are my own.

W. O'D.

WINTER GARDEN

Jardín de Invierno

EL EGOÍSTA

No falta nadie en el jardín. No hay nadie:
sólo el invierno verde y negro, el día
desvelado como una aparición,
fantasma blanco, fría vestidura,
por las escalas de un castillo. Es hora
de que no llegue nadie, apenas caen
las gotas que cuajaban el rocío
en las ramas desnudas del invierno
y yo y tú en esta zona solitaria,
invencibles y solos, esperando
que nadie llegue, no, que nadie venga
con sonrisa o medalla o presupuesto
a proponernos nada.

Ésta es la hora
de las hojas caídas, trituradas
sobre la tierra, cuando
de ser y de no ser vuelven al fondo
despojándose de oro y de verdura
hasta que son raíces otra vez
y otra vez, demoliéndose y naciendo,
suben a conocer la primavera.

Oh corazón perdido
en mí mismo, en mi propia investidura,
qué generosa transición te puebla!
Yo no soy el culpable
de haber huido ni de haber acudido:
no me pudo gastar la desventura!
La propia dicha puede ser amarga
a fuerza de besarle cada día

THE EGOIST

Nobody is missing from the garden. Nobody is here:
only the green and black winter, the day
waking from sleep like a ghost,
a white phantom in cold garments
climbing the steps of a castle. It's an hour
when no one should arrive. Just a few drops
of chilly dew keep falling
from the bare branches of winter
and you and I in this circle of solitude,
invincible and alone, waiting
for no one to arrive, no, nobody will come
with a smile or a medal or a budget
to make us an offer or ask for anything.

This is the hour
of fallen leaves, their dust
scattered over the earth, when
they return to the depths of being and not being
and abandon the gold and the greenery,
until they are roots again,
and again, torn down and being born,
they rise up to know the spring.

O heart lost
inside me, in this man's essence,
what bountiful change inhabits you!
I am not the culprit
who has fled or turned himself in:
misery could not exhaust me!
Your own happiness can grow bitter
if you kiss it every day,

3

y no hay camino para liberarse
del sol sino la muerte.

Qué puedo hacer si me escogió la estrella
para relampaguear, y si la espina
me condujo al dolor de algunos muchos.
Qué puedo hacer si cada movimiento
de mi mano me acercó a la rosa?
Debo pedir perdón por este invierno,
el más lejano, el más inalcanzable
para aquel hombre que buscaba el frío
sin que sufriera nadie por su dicha?

Y si entre estos caminos
— Francia distante, números de niebla —
vuelvo al recinto de mi propia vida:
un jardín solo, una comuna pobre,
y de pronto este día igual a todos
baja por las escalas que no existen
vestido de pureza irresistible,
y hay un olor de soledad aguda,
de humedad, de agua, de nacer de nuevo:
qué puedo hacer si respiro sin nadie,
por qué voy a sentirme malherido?

and there is no way of freeing oneself
from the sunlight except to die.

What can I do if the star chose me
to flash with lightning, and if the thorn
guided me to the pain of so many others.
What can I do if every movement
of my hand brought me closer to the rose?
Should I beg forgiveness for this winter,
the most distant, the most unattainable
for that man who used to seek out the chill
without anyone suffering because of his happiness?

And if somewhere on those roads:
— distant France, numerals of fog —
I return to the extent of my life:
a lonely garden, a poor district,
and suddenly this day equal to all others
descends the stairs that do not exist
dressed in irresistible purity,
and there is the odor of sharp solitude,
of humidity, of water, of being born again:
what can I do if I breathe my own air,
why will I feel wounded to death?

GAUTAMA CRISTO

Los nombres de Dios y en particular de su representante
llamado Jesús o Cristo, según textos y bocas,
han sido usados, gastados y dejados
a la orilla del río de las vidas
como las conchas vacías de un molusco.
Sin embargo, al tocar estos nombres sagrados
y desangrados, pétalos heridos,
saldos de los océanos del amor y del miedo,
algo aún permanece: un labio de ágata,
una huella irisada que aún tiembla en la luz.

Mientras se usaban los nombres de Dios
por los mejores y por los peores, por los limpios y por los sucios
por los blancos y los negros, por ensangrentados asesinos
y por las víctimas doradas que ardieron en napalm,
mientras Nixon con las manos
de Caín bendecía a sus condenados a muerte,
mientras menos y menores huellas divinas se hallaron en la playa,
los hombres comenzaron a estudiar los colores,
el porvenir de la miel, el signo del uranio,
buscaron con desconfianza y esperanza las posibilidades
de matarse y de no matarse, de organizarse en hileras,
de ir más allá, de ilimitarse sin reposo.

Los que cruzamos estas edades con gusto a sangre,
a humo de escombros, a ceniza muerta,
y no fuimos capaces de perder la mirada,
a menudo nos detuvimos en los nombres de Dios,

GAUTAMA CHRIST

The names of God and especially of his representative
called Jesus or Christ, according to texts and mouths,
have been used up, worn down and deposited
on the riverbank of our lives
like empty mollusk shells.
Nevertheless, touching these sacred names
drained of their blood, wounded petals,
balances of the oceans of love and of fear,
we know something endures there: an agate lip,
an irridescent footprint still shimmering in the light.

While the names of God were spoken
by the best and the worst, by the clean and the dirty,
by whites and blacks, by blood-stained assassins
and golden brown victims who blazed with napalm,
while Nixon with the hands
of Cain blessed those he had condemned to death,
when fewer and smaller divine footprints were found on the beach,
men began to examine the colors,
the promise of honey, the symbol for uranium,
with suspicion and hope they studied the possibilities
of killing and not killing each other, of organizing themselves in rows,
of going even further, of making themselves limitless, without rest.

We who live through these ages with their bloody flavor,
the smell of smoking rubble, of dead ash,
we who were not able to forget the sight
have often stopped to think in the names of God,

los levantamos con ternura porque nos recordaban
a los antecesores, a los primeros, a los que interrogaron,
a los que encontraron el himno que los unió en la desdicha
y ahora viendo los fragmentos vacíos donde habitó aquel hombre
sentimos estas suaves sustancias
gastadas, malgastadas por la bondad y por la maldad.

have raised them up tenderly, because they reminded us
of our ancestors, of the first humans, of those who asked questions,
of those who found the hymn that united them in misery
and now seeing the empty fragments where that man lived
we finger those smooth substances
spent, squandered by good and evil.

LA PIEL DEL ABEDUL

Como la piel del abedul
eres plateada y olorosa:
tengo que contar con tus ojos
al describir la primavera.

Y aunque no sé cómo te llamas
no hay primer tomo sin mujer:
los libros se escriben con besos
(y yo les ruego que se callen
para que se acerque la lluvia).

Quiero decir que entre dos mares
está colgando mi estatura
como una bandera abatida.
Y por mi amada sin mirada
estoy dispuesto hasta a morir
aunque mi muerte se atribuya
a mi deficiente organismo
o a la tristeza innecesaria
depositada en los roperos.
Lo cierto es que el tiempo se escapa
y con voz de viuda me llama
desde los bosques olvidados.

Antes de ver el mundo, entonces,
cuando mis ojos no se abrían
yo disponía de cuatro ojos:
los míos y los de mi amor:
no me pregunten si he cambiado:
(es sólo el tiempo el que envejece):

THE SKIN OF BIRCH

Like the skin of a birch
you are silvery and fragrant:
I must rely upon your eyes
to describe spring.

And though I do not know your name
without woman there'd be no first book:
those books are written with kisses
(and I beg them to be silent
so I can hear the rain).

I want to say how between two seas
my whole being hangs
like a disheartened flag.
And for my blind beloved
I am ready to die
though my death will be blamed
on my deficient organism
or on the unnecessary sadness
deposited in clothes closets.
The truth is, time escapes
and with a widow's voice calls me
from the forgotten woods.

Before I saw the world, then,
when my eyes still hadn't opened,
I already had four eyes:
my own and my beloved's:
don't ask me if I have changed:
(time is the only one who grows old):

(vive cambiando de camisa
mientras yo sigo caminado).

Todos los labios del amor
fueron haciendo mi ropaje
desde que me sentí desnudo:
ella se llamaba María
(tal vez Teresa se llamaba),
y me acostumbré a caminar
consumido por mis pasiones.

Eres tú la que tú serás
mujer innata de mi amor,
la que de greda fue formada
o la de plumas que voló
o la mujer territorial
de cabellera en el follaje
o la concéntrica caída
como una moneda desnuda
en el estanque de un topacio
o la presente cuidadora
de mi incorrecta indisciplina
o bien la que nunca nació
y que yo espero todavía.

Porque la luz del abedul
es la piel de la primavera.

(he's always changing his shirt
while I go on walking).

All love's lips
made my clothes
when I felt naked:
she was called Maria
(or maybe her name was Teresa)
and I grew used to walking
consumed by my passion.

You are who you will be
woman born in my love,
the one formed from clay
or the feathered one who flew
or that woman bound to earth
with her hair in the leaves
or the concentric one who fell
like a naked coin
in the pool of a topaz
or the current caretaker
of my brazen indolent ways
or perhaps a woman who was never born
and for whom I am still waiting.

Because the birch tree's light
is the skin of spring.

MODESTAMENTE

Hay que conocer ciertas virtudes
normales, vestimentas de cada día
que de tanto ser vistas paracen invisibles
y no entregarnos al excepcional,
al tragafuego o a la mujer araña.

Sin duda que preconizo la excelencia silvestre,
el respeto anticuado, la sede natural,
la economía de los hechos sublimes que se pegan
de roca en roca a las generaciones sucesivas,
como ciertos moluscos vencedores del mar.

Toda la gente, somos nosotros, los eslabones grises
de las vidas que se repiten hasta la muerte,
y no llevamos uniformes desmesurados, ni rupturas precisas:
nos convienen las comunicaciones, el limpio amor, el pan puro,
el fútbol, las calles atravesadas con basuras a la puerta,
los perros de condescendientes colas, el jugo de un limón
en el advenimiento del pescado pacífico.

Pido autorización para ser como todos,
como todo el mundo y también, como cualquiera:
le ruego a usted, encarecidamente,
si se trata de mí, ya que de eso se trata,
que se elimine el cornetazo durante mi visita
y se resignen ustedes a mi tranquila ausencia.

MODESTLY

We are supposed to know certain common
virtues, vestments for each day of the week
that we see so often they become invisible
and do not surrender us to the mysterious,
to the fire swallower or the spider woman.

Without doubt I praise the wild excellence,
the old fashioned reverence, the natural see,
the economy of sublime truths that cling
to rock upon rock in succeeding generations,
like certain mollusks who conquered the sea.

We are all the people, the gray links
of lives that repeat themselves until death,
and we never wear unfitting uniforms, no precise tears:
it's proper that we communicate, have clean love, pure bread,
soccer, side streets with garbage in the doorways,
the dogs with complacent tails, the juice of a lemon
with the arrival of the peaceful fish.

I ask permission to be like everybody else,
like the rest of the world and what's more, like anybody else:
I beg you, with all my heart,
if we are talking about me, since we are talking about me,
please resist blasting the trumpet during my visit
and resign yourselves to my quiet absence.

CON QUEVEDO, EN PRIMAVERA

Todo ha florecido en
estos campos, manzanos,
azules titubeantes, malezas amarillas,
y entre la hierba verde viven las amapolas.
El cielo inextinguible, el aire nuevo
de cada día, el tácito fulgor,
regalo de una extensa primavera.
Sólo no hay primavera en mi recinto.
Enfermedades, besos desquiciados,
como yedras de iglesia se pegaron
a las ventanas negras de mi vida
y el sólo amor no basta, ni el salvaje
y extenso aroma de la primavera.

Y para ti qué son en este ahora
la luz desenfrenada, el desarrollo
floral de la evidencia, el canto verde
de las verdes hojas, la presencia
del cielo con su copa de frescura?
Primavera exterior, no me atormentes,
desatando en mis brazos vino y nieve,
corola y ramo roto de pesares,
dame por hoy el sueño de las hojas
nocturnas, la noche en que se encuentran
los muertos, los metales, las raíces,
y tantas primaveras extinguidas
que despiertan en cada primavera.

Everything has flowered in
these fields, apple trees,
hesitant blues, yellow weeds,
and in green grass the poppies thrive.
The inextinguishable sky, the new air
of each day, the invisible shine within,
that gift of a wide and vast springtime.
But spring hasn't come to my room.
Diseases, dubious kisses,
that stuck like the church's ivy
to the black windows of my life
and love alone is never enough, not even the wild
and expansive fragrance of spring.

And, to you, what can these mean now:
the orgiastic light, the evidence unfolding
like a flower, the green song
in the green leaves, the presence
of the sky with its goblet of freshness?
External spring, do not torment me,
unleashing wine and snow in my arms,
corolla and battered bouquet of sorrow,
just for today give me the sleep of nocturnal
leaves, the night of the dead, the metals, the roots,
and so many extinguished springtimes
that awaken to life every spring.

TODOS SABER

Alguien preguntará más tarde, alguna vez
buscando un nombre, el suyo o cualquier otro nombre,
por qué desestimé su amistad o su amor
o su razón o su delirio o sus trabajos:
tendrá razón: fue mi deber nombrarte,
a ti, al de más allá y al de más cerca,
a alguno por la heroica cicatriz,
a la mujer aquella por su pétalo,
al arrogante por su inocencia agresiva,
al olvidado por su oscuridad insigne.

Pero no tuve tiempo ni tinta para todos.

O bien el menoscabo de la ciudad, del tiempo,
el frío corazón de los relojes
que latieron cortando mi medida,
algo pasó, no descifré,
no alcancé todos los significados:
pido perdón al que no está presente:
mi obligación fue comprender a todos, delirante,
débil, tenaz, manchado, heroico, vil,
amante hasta las lágrimas, ingrato,
redentor atrapado en su cadena,
enlutado campeón de la alegría.

Ay, para qué contamos tus verdades
si yo viví con ellas,
si yo soy cada uno y cada vez,
si yo me llamo siempre con tu nombre.

FOR ALL TO KNOW

Someone will ask later, sometimes
searching for a name, his own or someone else's,
why I neglected his sadness or his love
or his reason or his delirium or his hardships:
and he'll be right: it was my duty to name you,
you, someone far away and someone close by,
to name someone for his heroic scar,
to name a woman for her petal,
the arrogant one for his fierce innocence,
the forgotten one for his famous obscurity.

But I didn't have enough time or ink for everyone.

Or maybe it was the strain of the city, of time,
the cold heart of the clocks
that beat interrupting my measure,
something happened, I didn't decipher it,
I couldn't grasp each and every meaning:
I ask forgiveness from anyone not here:
it was my duty to understand everybody, becoming delirious,
weak, unyielding, compromised, heroic, vile,
loving until I wept, and sometimes an ingrate,
a savior entangled in his own chains,
all dressed in black, toasting to joy.

Why describe your truths
if I lived with them,
I am everybody and every time,
I always call myself by your name.

IMAGEN

De una mujer que apenas conocí
guardo el nombre cerrado: es una caja,
alzo de tarde en tarde las sílabas que tienen
herrumbre y crujen como pianos desvencijados:
salen luego los árboles aquellos, de la lluvia,
los jazmines, las trenzas victoriosas
de una mujer sin cuerpo ya, perdida,
ahogada en el tiempo como en un lento lago:
sus ojos se apagaron allí como carbones.

Sin embargo, hay en la disolución
fragancia muerta, arterias enterradas,
o simplemente vida entre otras vidas.

Es aromático volver el rostro
sin otra dirección que la pureza:
tomar el pulso al cielo torrencial
de nuestra juventud menoscabada:
girar un anillo al vacío,
poner el grito en el cielo.

Siento no tener tiempo para mis existencias,
la mínima, el souvenir dejado en un vagón
de tren, en una alcoba o en la cervecería,
como un paraguas que allí se quedó en la lluvia:
tal vez son estos labios imperceptibles
los que se escuchan como resonancia marina
de pronto, en un descuido del camino.

IMAGE

I am keeping the name of a woman
I barely knew locked up: it's in a box,
and now and then I pick out the syllables
that are rusted and creak like rickety pianos:
soon those trees come out, and then the rain,
the jasmine, the long victorious braids
of a woman now without a body, lost,
drowned in time as in a slow lake:
there her eyes went out like coals.

Nevertheless, there is in dissolution
the sweet scent of death, buried arteries,
or simply a life among other lives.

It smells good to turn our face
only in the direction of purity:
to feel the pulse of the raining sky
of our diminished youth:
to twirl a ring in the emptiness,
to cry out to heaven.

I regret not having time for my lives,
even for the slightest thing, the souvenir left in a compartment
of a train, in a bedroom or at the brewery,
like an umbrella left there in the rain:
perhaps these are the imperceptible lips
that speak like the cadence of the sudden
sea, in a careless moment on the road.

Por eso, Irene o Rosa, María o Leonor,
cajas vacías, flores secas dentro de un libro,
llaman en circunstancias solitarias
y hay que abrir, hay que oír lo que no tiene voz,
hay que ver estas cosas que no existen.

For that reason, Irene or Rose, Mary or Leonore,
empty boxes, dry flowers pressed in a book,
they call out from their lonely corners
and we need to open them, to hear the one without a voice,
to see those things that do not exist.

LLAMA EL OCÉANO

No voy al mar en este ancho verano
cubierto de calor, no voy más lejos
de los muros, las puertas y las grietas
que circundan las vidas y mi vida.

En qué distancia, frente a cuál ventana,
en qué estación de trenes
dejé olvidado el mar y allí quedamos,
yo dando las espaldas a lo que amo
mientras allá seguía la batalla
de blanco y verde y piedra y centelleo.

Así fue, así parece que así fue:
cambian las vidas, y el que va muriendo
no sabe que esa parte de la vida,
esa nota mayor, esa abundancia
de cólera y fulgor quedaron lejos,
te fueron ciegamente cercenadas.

No, yo me niego al mar desconocido,
muerto, rodeado de ciudades tristes,
mar cuyas olas no saben matar,
ni cargarse de sal y de sonido:
Yo quiero el mío mar, la artillería
del océano golpeando las orillas,
aquel derrumbe insigne de turquesas,
la espuma donde muere el poderío.

No salgo al mar este verano: estoy
encerrado, enterrado, y a lo largo

THE OCEAN CALLS

I am not going to the sea in this long summer
covered with heat, I'm not going any farther
than the walls, the doors and the cracks
that surround other lives and my life.

In which distance, facing what window,
in which train station
did I leave the sea forgotten, and there we were left,
I turning my back on those things I love
while there the struggle went on and on
of white and green and stone and glimmer.

So it went, at least that's the way it seems:
lives change, and he who has begun to die
doesn't know that that side of life,
that major chord, that abundance
of rage and splendor were left in the distance,
they were blindly sliced away from you.

Yes, I deny myself the unknown sea,
dead, surrounded by saddened cities,
sea whose waves never learn to kill
and never fill up with salt and sound:
I want my sea, the artillery
of the ocean that strikes the shore,
that lustrous turquoise tumbling,
the spume in which power dies.

I'm not going to the sea this summer: I am
shut in, buried, and inside the length

del túnel que me lleva prisionero
oigo remotamente un trueno verde,
un cataclismo de botellas rotas,
un susurro de sal y de agonía.

Es el libertador. Es el océano,
lejos, allá, en mi patria, que me espera.

of the tunnel that holds me prisoner
I faintly hear the green thunder,
a cataclysm of shattered bottles,
a whisper of salt and of agony.

The liberator lives. It is the ocean,
far away, there, in my motherland, that awaits me.

PÁJARO

Un pájaro elegante,
patas delgadas, cola interminable,
viene
cerca de mí, a saber qué animal soy.

Sucede en Primavera,
en Condé-sur-Iton, en Normandía.
Tiene una estrella o gota
de cuarzo, harina o nieve
en la frente minúscula
y dos rayas azules lo recorren
desde el cuello a la cola,
dos líneas estelares de turquesa.

Da minúsculos saltos
mirándome rodeado
de pasto verde y cielo
y son dos signos interrogativos
estos nerviosos ojos acechantes
como dos alfileres,
dos puntas negras, rayos diminutos
que me atraviesan para preguntarme
si vuelo y hacia dónde.
Intrépido, vestido
como una flor por sus ardientes plumas,
directo, decidido
frente a la hostilidad de mi estatura,

BIRD

An elegant bird,
slender feet, endless tail,
comes
close to me, to see what animal I am.

It happens in the spring,
in Condé-sur-Iton, in Normandy.
It has a star or drop
of quartz, flour or snow
on its tiny forehead
and two blue stripes run
from the neck to the tail,
two turquoise lines of stars.

It takes small hops
watching me surrounded
by green pasture and sky,
and they are two question marks
those nervous eyes waiting in ambush
like two pins,
two black points, thin rays of light
that stop me in my tracks and ask
if I fly and where to.
Fearless, dressed
like a flower in fiery feathers,
direct, determined
facing my tall threatening frame,

de pronto encuentra un grano o un gusano
y a saltos de delgados pies de alambre
abandona el enigma
de este gigante que se queda solo,
sin su pequeña vida pasajera.

suddenly it discovers a grain or a worm
and hopping away on thin wire feet
it abandons the mystery
of this giant who remains alone,
apart from its small, fleeting life.

JARDÍN DE INVIERNO

Llega el invierno. Espléndido dictado
me dan las lentas hojas
vestidas de silencio y amarillo.

Soy un libro de nieve,
una espaciosa mano, una pradera,
un círculo que espera,
pertenezco a la tierra y a su invierno.

Creció el rumor del mundo en el follaje,
ardió después el trigo constelado
por flores rojas como quemaduras,
luego llegó el otoño a establecer
la escritura del vino:
todo pasó, fue cielo pasajero
la copa del estío,
y se apagó la nube navegante.

Yo esperé en el balcón tan enlutado,
como ayer con las yedras de mi infancia,
que la tierra extendiera
sus alas en mi amor deshabitado.

Yo supe que la rosa caería
y el hueso del durazno transitorio
volvería a dormir y a germinar:
y me embriagué con la copa del aire
hasta que todo el mar se hizo nocturno
y el arrebol se convirtió en ceniza.

WINTER GARDEN

Winter arrives. Shining dictation
the wet leaves give me,
dressed in silence and yellow.

I am a book of snow,
a spacious hand, an open meadow,
a circle that waits,
I belong to the earth and its winter.

Earth's rumor grew in the leaves,
soon the wheat flared up
punctuated by red flowers like burns,
then autumn arrived to set down
the wine's scripture:
everything passed, the goblet of summer
was a fleeting sky,
the navigating cloud burned out.

I stood on the balcony dark with mourning,
like yesterday with the ivies of my childhood,
hoping the earth would spread its wings
in my uninhabited love.

I knew the rose would fall
and the pit of the passing peach
would sleep and germinate once more,
and I got drunk on the air
until the whole sea became the night
and the red sky turned to ash.

La tierra vive ahora
tranquilizando su interrogatorio,
extendida la piel de su silencio.
Yo vuelvo a ser ahora
el taciturno que llegó de lejos
envuelto en lluvia fría y en campanas:
debo a la muerte pura de la tierra
la voluntad de mis germinaciones.

Now the earth lives
numbing its oldest questions,
the skin of its silence stretched out.
Once more I am the silent one
who came out of the distance
wrapped in cold rain and bells:
I owe to earth's pure death
the will to sprout.

MUCHAS GRACIAS

Hay que andar tanto por el mundo
para constatar ciertas cosas,
ciertas leyes de sol azul,
el rumor central del dolor,
la exactitud primaveral.

Yo soy tardío de problemas:
llego tarde al anfiteatro
donde se espera la llegada
de la sopa de los centauros!
Allí brillan los vencedores
y se multiplica el otoño.

Por qué yo vivo desterrado
del esplendor de las naranjas?

Me he dado cuenta poco a poco
que en estos días sofocantes
se me va la vida en sentarme,
gasto la luz en las alfombras.

Si no me dejaron entrar
en la casa de los urgentes,
de los que llegaron a tiempo,
quiero saber lo que pasó
cuando se cerraron las puertas.

Cuando se cerraron las puertas
y el mundo desapareció

MANY THANKS

We have to walk a long way in the world
to know the truth of certain things,
certain laws of blue sunlight,
the inherent rumor of pain,
the precision of spring.

I procrastinate to a fault:
I arrive late at the amphitheatre
where everyone is awaiting the arrival
of the soup of the centaurs!
There the conquerors glitter
and autumn multiplies.

Why do I live exiled
from the shine of the oranges?

Little by little, I have realized
that during these suffocating days
life slips away as I sit here,
I waste light on the carpets.

Since they wouldn't let me enter
the house of the insistent crowd,
of those who arrived on time,
I want to know what happened
when they closed the doors.

When they closed the doors
and the world disappeared

en un murmullo de sombreros
que repetían como el mar
un prestigioso movimiento.

Con estas razones de ausencia
pido perdón por mi conducta.

in a fluttering of hats
that repeated like the sea
a grand illusion of motion.

With these excuses for my absence
I beg forgiveness for my ways.

REGRESOS

Dos regresos se unieron a mi vida
y al mar de cada día:
de una vez afronté la luz, la tierra,
cierta paz provisoria. Una cebolla
era la luna, globo
nutricio de la noche, el sol naranja
sumergido en el mar:
una llegada
que soporté, que reprimí hasta ahora,
que yo determiné, y aquí me quedo:
ahora la verdad es el regreso.

Lo sentí como quebrantadura,
como una nuez de vidrio
que se rompe en la roca
y por allí, en un trueno, entró la luz,
la luz del litoral, del mar perdido,
del mar ganado ahora y para siempre.

Yo soy el hombre de tanto regresos
que forman un racimo traicionado,
de nuevo, adiós, por un temible viaje
en que voy sin llegar a parte alguna:
mi única travesía es un regreso.

Y esta vez entre las incitaciones
temí tocar la arena, el resplandor
de este mar malherido y derramado,

HOMECOMINGS

Two homecomings sustained my life
and the daily sea, ebbing and rising:
at once I faced the light, the earth,
a certain provisional peace. The moon
was an onion, nourishing globe
of the night, the orange sun
submerged in the sea:
an arrival that
I endured and kept buried until now,
it was my will and here I shall remain:
now my homecoming is the truth.

I felt it as a blow,
like a crystal nut
shattering on a boulder
and in that way, in a thunderclap, the light flashed,
the light of the littoral, of the lost sea,
of the sea captured now and forever.

I am a man of so many homecomings
that form a cluster of betrayals,
and again, I leave on a frightening voyage
in which I travel and never arrive anywhere:
my single journey is a homecoming.

And this time among seductions
I was afraid to touch the sand, the sparkle
of this wounded and scattered sea,

pero dispuesto ya a mis injusticias
la decisión cayó con el sonido
de un fruto de cristal que se destroza
y en el golpe sonoro vi la vida,
la tierra envuelta en sombras y destellos
y la copa del mar bajo mis labios.

but accepting of my unjust acts
my decision fell with the sound
of a glass fruit that shatters
and in this resounding blow I glimpsed life,
the earth wrapped in shadows and sparks
and the cup of the sea below my lips.

LOS PERDIDOS DEL BOSQUE

Yo soy uno de aquellos que no alcanzó a llegar al bosque,
de los retrocedidos por el invierno en la tierra,
atajados por escarabajos de irisación y picadura
o por tremendos ríos que se oponían al destino.
Éste es el bosque, el follaje es cómodo, son altísimos muebles
los árboles, ensimismadas cítaras las hojas,
se borraron senderos, cercados, patrimonios,
el aire es patriarcal y tiene olor a tristeza.

Todo es ceremonioso en el jardín salvaje
de la infancia: hay manzanas cerca del agua
que llega de la nieve negra escondida en los Andes:
manzanas cuyo áspero rubor no conoce los dientes
del hombre, sino el picoteo de pájaros voraces,
manzanas que inventaron la simetría silvestre
y que caminan con lentísimo paso hacia el azúcar.

Todo es nuevo y antiguo en el esplendor circundante,
los que hasta aquí vinieron son los menoscabados,
y los que se quedaron atrás en la distancia
son los náufragos que pueden o no sobrevivir:
sólo entonces conocerán las leyes del bosque.

THE LOST ONES OF THE FOREST

I am someone who never made it to the forest,
one of those turned back by earth's winter,
headed off by lively scarabs ready to bite
or by tremendous rivers that opposed my destiny.
This is the forest, the thicket is comfortable, the trees
are the grandest furniture, the leaves vain zithers,
the trails, fenced pastures, estates were erased,
the air is patriarchal and smells of sadness.

Everything is ceremony in the wild garden
of childhood: apples sit beside the river
descended from black snow hidden in the Andes:
apples whose sour blush hasn't known the teeth
of men, only the pecking of ravenous birds,
apples that invented a natural symmetry
and move slowly toward sweetness.

Everything is new and old in the surrounding luster,
those who came here are the diminished ones,
and those who were left behind in the distance
are the shipwrecked who may or may not survive:
only then will they know the laws of the forest.

IN MEMORIAM MANUEL Y BENJAMÍN

Al mismo tiempo, dos de mi carrera,
de mi cantera, dos de mis trabajos,
se murieron con horas de intervalo:
uno envuelto en Santiago, el otro en Tacna:
dos singulares, sólo parecidos
ahora, única vez, porque se han muerto.

El primero fue taimado y soberano,
áspero, de rugosa investidura,
más bien dado al silencio:
de obrero trabajado conservó
la mano de tarea predispuesta
a la piedra, al metal de la herrería.
El otro, inquieto del conocimiento,
ave de rama en rama de la vida,
fuegocentrista como un bello faro
de intermitentes rayos.
                    Dos secuaces
de dos sabidurías diferentes:
dos nobles solitarios que hoy se unieron
para mí en la noticia de la muerte.

Amé a mis dos opuestos compañeros
que, enmudeciendo, me han dejado mudo
sin saber qué decir ni qué pensar.

Tanto buscar debajo de la piel
y tanto andar entre almas y raíces,
tanto picar papel hora tras hora!

IN MEMORY OF MANUEL AND BENJAMÍN

At the same time, two lives of my career,
two from my quarry, two of my labors,
died within hours of each other:
one shrouded in Santiago, the other in Tacna:
two singular beings who have something in common
now, at long last, because they have died.

The first one was somber and kingly,
harsh, with his rugged character,
and seldom spoke a word:
a hard laborer he kept hands
that were always ready to shape
the stone, to hammer the hot metal.
The other one, restless to know things,
a bird hopping branch to branch in life,
the fire at his center like a beautiful beacon
breaking into intermittent rays of light.
                                    Two partisans
following two separate visions:
two lonesome nobles who today came together
for me, at the news of their death.

I loved my two contrary friends
who, with their silence, left me speechless
without knowing what to think or say.

So much searching under the skin
and so much walking among souls and roots,
hour by hour so much pecking at paper.

Ahora quietos están, acostumbrándose
a un nuevo espacio de la oscuridad,
el uno con su rectitud de roble
y el otro con su espejo y espejismo:
los dos que se pasaron nuestras vidas
cortando el tiempo, escarmenando, abriendo
surcos, rastreando la palabra justa,
el pan de la palabra cada día.

(Si no tuvieron tiempo de cansarse
ahora quietos y por fin solemnes
entran compactos a este gran silencio ·
que desmenuzará sus estaturas.)

No se hicieron las lágrimas jamás
para estos hombres.
                    Y nuestras palabras
suenan a hueco como tumbas nuevas
donde nuestras pisadas desentonan,
mientras ellos allí se quedan solos,
con naturalidad, como existieron.

They are quiet now, settling into
a new sphere of darkness,
one with the rectitude of an oak tree,
the other with his mirror and his illusion:
those two who passed through our lives
chiseling time, untangling, opening
furrows, trailing the just word,
the bread of the word every day.

(Even if they didn't have the time to grow tired,
now quiet and finally solemn,
they enter, pressed together, the vast silence
that will slowly grind down their frames.)

Tears were never invented
for those men.
          And our words
sound as hollow as a new tomb
in which our footsteps sound out of key,
while they remain there alone,
naturally, as they existed.

EL TIEMPO

De muchos días se hace el día, una hora
tiene minutos atrasados que llegaron y el día
se forma con extravagantes olvidos, con metales,
cristales, ropa que siguió en los rincones,
predicciones, mensajes que no llegaron nunca.
El día es un estanque en el bosque futuro,
esperando, poblándose de hojas, de advertencias,
de sonidos opacos que entraron en el agua
como piedras celestes.
                    A la orilla
quedan las huellas doradas del zorro vespertino
que como un pequeño rey rápido quiere la guerra:
el día acumula en su luz briznas, murmullos:
todo surge de pronto como una vestidura
que es nuestra, es el fulgor acumulado
que aguardaba y que muere por orden de la noche
volcándose en la sombra.

TIME

The day is made from many days, an hour
keeps slow minutes that found their way, and the day
grows and grows with extravagant forgottens, with metals,
crystals, clothes still flung in the corners,
predictions, messages that never arrived.
The day is a pool in the future forest,
waiting, filling with leaves, with warnings,
with dark sounds that entered the water
like celestial stones.
                    On the bank
remain the golden footprints of the evening fox
who like a small impetuous king wants war:
the day collects in threads of light, in murmurs:
it all suddenly springs up like a vestment
that belongs to us, it is the collective shine
that waited and dies on the orders of the night
splashing in the shadows.

ANIMAL DE LUZ

Soy en este sin fin sin soledad
un animal de luz acorralado
por sus errores y por su follaje:
ancha es la selva: aquí mis semejantes
pululan, retroceden o trafican,
mientras yo me retiro acompañado
por la escolta que el tiempo determina:
olas del mar, estrellas de la noche.

Es poco, es ancho, es escaso y es todo.
De tanto ver mis ojos otros ojos
y mi boca de tanto ser besada,
de haber tragado el humo
de aquellos trenes desaparecidos:
las viejas estaciones despiadadas
y el polvo de incesantes librerías,
el hombre yo, el mortal, se fatigó
de ojos, de besos, de humo, de caminos,
de libros más espesos que la tierra.

Y hoy en el fondo del bosque perdido
oye el rumor del enemigo y huye
no de los otros sino de sí mismo,
de la conversación interminable,
del coro que cantaba con nosotros
y del significado de la vida.

Porque una vez, porque una voz, porque una
sílaba o el transcurso de un silencio

ANIMAL OF LIGHT

I am in this endless lack of solitude
an animal of light corralled
by his mistakes and by his foliage:
the forest is wide: here my brother creatures
swarm, back away or roam around,
while I retreat accompanied
by the escort that time chooses:
waves of the sea, stars of the night.

It is small, it is wide, scarce and is everything.
My eyes from looking into so many eyes
and my mouth from so many kisses,
from having swallowed the smoke
of those trains that vanished:
the old merciless stations
and the dust of countless bookshops,
the man I am, the mortal, weary
of eyes, of kisses, of smoke, of roads,
tired of books thicker than the earth.

And today, deep in the lost forest
he hears the rustling of the enemy and flees
not from the others but from himself,
from the interminable conversation,
from the choir that used to sing with us
and from the meaning of life.

Because one moment, because one voice, because one
syllable or the passing of one silence

o el sonido insepulto de la ola
me dejan frente a frente a la verdad,
y no hay nada más que descifrar,
ni nada más que hablar: eso era todo:
se cerraron las puertas de la selva,
circula el sol abriendo los follajes,
sube la luna como fruta blanca
y el hombre se acomoda a su destino.

or the undying sound of the wave
leave me face to face with the truth,
and there is nothing left to decipher,
nothing more to say: that was all:
the doors of the forest are closed,
the sun circles opening the leaves,
the moon rises like a white fruit
and man suits himself to his destiny.

LOS TRIÁNGULOS

Tres triángulos de pájaros cruzaron
sobre el enorme océano extendido
en el invierno como una bestia verde.
Todo yace, el silencio,
el desarrollo gris, la luz pesada
del espacio, la tierra intermitente.
Por encima de todo fue pasando
un vuelo
y otro vuelo
de aves oscuras, cuerpos invernales,
triángulos temblorosos
cuyas alas
agitándose apenas
llevan de un sitio a otro
de las costas de Chile
el frío gris, los desolados días.

Yo estoy aquí mientras de cielo en cielo
el temblor de las aves migratorias
me deja hundido en mí y en mi materia
como en un pozo de perpetuidad
cavado por una espiral inmóvil.

Ya desaparecieron:
plumas negras del mar,
pájaros férreos
de acantilados y de roqueríos,
ahora, a medio día

THE TRIANGLES

Three triangles of birds crossed
the enormous ocean stretched out
in winter like a single green beast.
Everything lies flat, the silence,
the extended gray, the heavy light
of the sky, the intermittent earth.
Over everything passed
one flight
and another flight
of dark birds, wintry bodies,
trembling triangles
whose wings
just barely moving
carry from one place to the next
on the coasts of Chile
the gray chill, the desolate days.

I am here while from sky to sky
the shiver of migrating birds
leaves me sunk in myself and in my flesh
as in a deep well of perpetuity
dug by a motionless spiral.

They have already disappeared:
black feathers of the sea,
iron birds
of steep cliffs and of rookeries,
now, at midday

frente al vacío estoy: es el espacio
del invierno extendido
y el mar se ha puesto
sobre el rostro azul
una máscara amarga.

I face the emptiness I am: it is the body
of winter stretched out
and the sea has slipped
over its blue face
a bitter mask.

UN PERRO HA MUERTO

Mi perro ha muerto.

Lo enterré en el jardín
junto a una vieja máquina oxidada.

Allí, no más abajo,
ni más arriba,
se juntará conmigo alguna vez.
Ahora él ya se fue con su pelaje,
su mala educación, su nariz fría.
Y yo, materialista que no cree
en el celeste cielo prometido
para ningún humano,
para este perro o para todo perro
creo en el cielo, sí, creo en un cielo
donde yo no entraré, pero él me espera
ondulando su cola de abanico
para que yo al llegar tenga armistades.

Ay no diré la tristeza en la tierra
de no tenerlo más por compañero
que para mí jamás fue un servidor.
Tuvo hacia mí la amistad de un erizo
que conservaba su soberanía,
la amistad de una estrella independiente
sin más intimidad que la precisa,
sin exageraciones:
no se trepaba sobre mi vestuario
llenándome de pelos o de sarna,
no se frotaba contra mi rodilla

A DOG HAS DIED

My dog has died.

I buried him in the garden
beside a rusty old engine.

There, not too deep,
not too shallow,
he will greet me sometime.
He already left with his coat,
his bad manners, his cold nose.
And I, a materialist who does not believe
in the starry heaven promised
to a human being,
for this dog and for every dog
I believe in heaven, yes, I believe in a heaven
that I will never enter, but he waits for me
wagging his big fan of a tail
so I, soon to arrive, will feel welcomed.

No, I will not speak about my sadness on earth
at not having him as a companion anymore,
he never stooped to becoming my servant.
He offered me the friendship of a sea urchin
who always kept his sovereignty,
the friendship of an independent star
with no more intimacy than necessary,
with no exaggerations:
he never used to climb over my clothes
covering me with hair or with mange,
he never used to rub against my knee

como otros perros obsesos sexuales.
No, mi perro me miraba
dándome la atención que necesito,
la atención necesaria
para hacer comprender a un vanidoso
que siendo perro él,
con esos ojos, más puros que los míos,
perdía el tiempo, pero me miraba
con la mirada que me reservó
toda su dulce, su peluda vida,
su silenciosa vida,
cerca de mí, sin molestarme nunca,
y sin pedirme nada.

Ay cuántas veces quise tener cola
andando junto a él por las orillas
del mar, en el Invierno de Isla Negra,
en la gran soledad: arriba el aire
traspasado de pájaros glaciales
y mi perro brincando, hirsuto, lleno
de voltaje marino en movimiento:
mi perro vagabundo y olfatorio
enarbolando su cola dorada
frente a frente al Océano y su espuma.

Alegre, alegre, alegre
como los perros saben ser felices,
sin nada más, con el absolutismo
de la naturaleza descarada.
No hay adiós a mi perro que se ha muerto.
Y no hay ni hubo mentira entre nosotros.

Ya se fue y lo enterré, y eso era todo.

like other dogs, obsessed with sex.
No, my dog used to watch me
giving me the attention I need,
yet only the attention necessary
to let a vain person know
that he being a dog,
with those eyes, more pure than mine,
was wasting time, but he watched
with a look that reserved for me
every bit of sweetness, his shaggy life,
his silent life,
sitting nearby, never bothering me,
never asking anything of me.

O, how many times I wanted to have a tail
walking next to him on the seashore,
in the Isla Negra winter,
in the vast solitude: above us
glacial birds pierced the air
and my dog frolicking, bristly hair, full
of the sea's voltage in motion:
my dog wandering and sniffing around,
brandishing his golden tail
in the face of the ocean and its spume.

O merry, merry, merry,
like only dogs know how to be happy
and nothing more, with an absolute
shameless nature.
There are no goodbyes for my dog who has died.
And there never were and are no lies between us.

He has gone and I buried him, and that was all.

OTOÑO

Estos meses arrastran la estridencia
de una guerra civil no declarada.
Hombres, mujeres, gritos, desafíos,
mientras se instala en la ciudad hostil,
en las arenas ahora desoladas
del mar y sus espumas verdaderas,
el Otoño, vestido de soldado,
gris de cabeza, lento de actitud:
el Otoño invasor cubre la tierra.

Chile despierta o duerme. Sale el sol
meditativo entre hojas amarillas
que vuelan como párpados políticos
desprendidos del cielo atormentado.

Si antes no había sitio por las calles,
ahora sí, la sustancia solitaria
de ti y de mí, tal vez de todo el mundo,
quiere salir de compras o de sueños,
busca el rectángulo de soledad
con el árbol aún verde que vacila
antes de deshojarse y desplomarse
vestido de oro y luego de mendigo.

Yo vuelvo al mar envuelto por el cielo:
el silencio entre una y otra ola
establece un suspenso peligroso:
muere la vida, se aquieta la sangre
hasta que rompe el nuevo movimiento
y resuena la voz del infinito.

AUTUMN

These months shriek and grate
like an undeclared civil war.
Men, women, screams, challenges,
while it occupies the hostile city,
the now deserted sandy beaches,
the ever-faithful foams and waves,
Autumn, dressed like a soldier,
its gray head, its slow march:
invader Autumn covers the earth.

Chile wakes or sleeps. A meditative sun
rises among the yellow leaves
that blow past like political eyelids
fallen from the tortured sky.

If there wasn't room in the crowded streets,
there is now, the solitary substance
of you and of me, maybe of everyone,
wants to go shopping or to dream,
searches for that rectangle of solitude
with the still green tree that sways
before losing its leaves and falling,
dressed in gold and later like a beggar.

I fly back to the sea wrapped in the sky:
the silence between one wave and the next
creates a terrifying suspense:
life ebbs out, blood stops flowing
until the new wave crashes on
and we hear the booming voice of infinity.

LA ESTRELLA

Bueno, ya no volví, ya no padezco
de no volver, se decidió la arena
y como parte de ola y de pasaje,
sílaba de la sal, piojo del agua,
yo, soberano, esclavo de la costa
me sometí, me encadené a mi roca.
No hay albedrío para los que somos
fragmento del asombro,
no hay salida para este volver
a uno mismo, a la piedra de uno mismo,
ya no hay más estrella que el mar.

THE STAR

Well, I never went back, I no longer suffer
from not going back, the sand willed it
and as part wave and part channel,
syllable of salt, leech of water,
I, sovereign, slave of the coast
surrendered, chained to my rock.
There is no freedom anymore for us
who are fragments of the mystery,
there is no way out for returning
to oneself, to the stone of oneself,
no other stars remain except the sea.

ABOUT THE TRANSLATOR

William O'Daly has been translating Spanish language
poetry for the last twelve years, concentrating on Pablo
Neruda's work since 1976. Copper Canyon Press pub-
lished his previous translations of Neruda, *Aún* (*Still
Another Day*, 1984) and *La Rosa Separada* (*The Sepa-
rate Rose*, 1985), and a limited edition of his own poems,
The Whale in the Web (1979).